LEOPARD ON
THE MOUNTAIN

For the children who have grown up under
my roof – Rakesh, Mukesh and Dolly – and for
Rakesh's children, Siddarth and Shristi
– a tale of the mountains we love so well . . .

**Other Cambridge Reading books
you may enjoy** ·

Leaving the Island Judith O'Neill

Clyde's Leopard Helen Dunmore

A True Spell and a Dangerous Susan Price

**Other books by Ruskin Bond
you may enjoy**

Earthquake

Ghost Trouble / Snake Trouble

Tiger Roars / Eagle Soars

Leopard on the Mountain

Ruskin Bond

Illustrated by Duncan Smith

CAMBRIDGE
UNIVERSITY PRESS

Cambridge Reading

General Editors
Richard Brown and Kate Ruttle

Consultant Editor
Jean Glasberg

PUBLISHED BY THE PRESS SYNDICATE OF THE UNIVERSITY OF CAMBRIDGE
The Pitt Building, Trumpington Street, Cambridge CB2 1RP, United Kingdom

CAMBRIDGE UNIVERSITY PRESS
The Edinburgh Building, Cambridge CB2 2RU, United Kingdom
40 West 20th Street, New York, NY 10011-4211, USA
10 Stamford Road, Oakleigh, Melbourne 3166, Australia

Text © Ruskin Bond 1998
Illustrations © Duncan Smith 1998

First published 1998

Printed in the United Kingdom at the University Press, Cambridge

Typeset in Concorde

A catalogue record for this book is available from the British Library

ISBN 0 521 47704 2

Contents

CHAPTER ONE

Five Miles to School

A leopard drank at the mountain stream, and then lay down on the grass to bask in the late February sunshine. Its tail twitched occasionally and the animal appeared to be sleeping. At the sound of distant voices it raised its head to listen, then stood up and leapt lightly over the boulders in the stream, disappearing among the trees on the opposite bank.

A minute or two later, three children, a girl and two boys, came walking down the forest path. Their school satchels looked new, their clothes had been washed and pressed. They were singing an old song they had learnt from their grandparents.

Five more miles to go!
We climb through rain and snow.
A river to cross –
A mountain to pass –
Now we've four more miles to go!

Their loud and cheerful singing startled a spotted forktail. The bird left its favourite rock in the stream and flew down the dark ravine.

"Well, we have only three more miles to go," said the bigger boy, Prakash, who had been this way hundreds of times. "But first, we have to cross the stream."

He was a sturdy twelve-year-old with eyes like blackcurrants and a mop of bushy hair that refused to settle down on his head. The girl and her young brother, Sonu, were taking this path for the first time.

"I'm tired, Bina," said Sonu.

Bina smiled at him, and Prakash said, "Don't worry, you'll get used to the walk." He glanced at the old watch he'd been given by his grandfather. "We can rest here for five or six minutes."

They sat down on a smooth boulder and watched the clear water of the shallow stream tumbling downhill. Bina examined the old watch on Prakash's wrist. The glass was badly scratched and she could barely make out the figures on the dial. "Are you sure that watch still gives the right time?" she asked.

"Well, it loses five minutes every day, so I put it ten minutes forward at night. That means by morning it's quite accurate. Even our teacher, Mr Mani, asks me for the time because the clock in our classroom keeps stopping. And if he doesn't ask, I tell him!"

They removed their shoes and let the cold mountain water run over their feet. Sonu pointed at some tracks in the sand and said they

were a leopard's, but Bina and Prakash paid no attention to him. None of the children had ever seen a leopard.

Bina was the same age as Prakash. She had pink cheeks, soft brown eyes, and hair that was just beginning to lose its natural curls. Hers was a gentle face, but a determined little chin hinted at the strength of her character. Sonu, her younger brother, was ten. He was a thin boy who had been sickly as a child but was now beginning to fill out. Although he didn't look very athletic, he could run like the wind.

Bina's primary school had been in her own village, Koli, but to reach her new school in Nauti, on the other side of the mountain, she would have to walk several miles every day. Sonu was changing schools too, just to keep Bina company. Prakash, their neighbour in Koli, had already been at school in Nauti for some time. His mischievous nature sometimes got him into trouble, and had resulted in his having to repeat a year, but this didn't seem to bother him at all.

"You'd rather look after your cows than go to

school, wouldn't you?" said Bina, as they got up to continue their walk.

"Oh, school's all right. Wait till you see old Mr Mani. He gets our names mixed up *and* the subjects he's supposed to be teaching. On the last day before the holidays he gave us geography when we were supposed to be doing maths!"

"Geography's more fun than maths," said Bina.

"There's a new teacher starting this year. They say she's very young, just out of college. I wonder what she'll be like."

Bina and Prakash walked fast, and Sonu had some trouble keeping up with them. Bina was excited about her new school, about going to this big village and meeting lots of different people. She had rarely been outside her own village, with its small school and single shop. There, the day's routine seldom varied – helping her mother in the fields after school, perhaps cutting grass and fodder for the cattle, or helping with household tasks like fetching water from the spring. Her father, who was a soldier, was away for nine months in the year and Sonu was still too frail to do the heavier tasks.

As the three children neared Nauti village,
they were joined by other children coming from
different directions, down little lanes and short-
cuts. These narrow paths zigzagged around the

hills and villages, cutting through fields and crossing narrow ravines. They came together to form a busy road along which mules, cattle and goats joined the throng.

Prakash knew almost everyone in the area, and exchanged greetings and gossip with labourers working on the road, with muleteers, bus drivers and milkmen, and with other children that they met along the way. He loved telling everyone the time, even if they didn't want to know.

As Prakash and his friends approached Nauti, the small, flat school buildings came into view on the outskirts of the village, fringed by a line of long-leaved pines. A small crowd had assembled on the single playing field. Something unusual seemed to be happening. Prakash ran forward to see what it was all about. Bina and Sonu stood aside, waiting in a patch of sunlight near the boundary wall.

Prakash soon came running back to them. He was bubbling over with excitement.

"It's old Mr Mani!" he gasped. "He's disappeared! They're saying a leopard must have carried him off!"

CHAPTER TWO

A Teacher Disappears

Mr Mani wasn't *really* old – he was only about fifty-five. But to the children, most adults over forty seemed ancient. And Mr Mani was absent-minded.

He had gone out for his early morning walk, saying he'd be back by eight o'clock, in time to have his breakfast and get ready for class. He lived with his sister and her husband, and when it was past nine, his sister presumed he'd stopped at a neighbour's house for breakfast (he loved tucking into other people's breakfasts) and that he had gone on to school from there. But when, at almost ten o'clock, Mr Mani still hadn't turned up at the school, questions were asked and guesses were made.

No-one had seen him return from his walk, and enquiries made in the village showed that he hadn't stopped at anyone's house. For Mr Mani to disappear was puzzling; for him to disappear without his breakfast was extraordinary.

Then a forest ranger returning from the next
village said he had seen a leopard sitting on a
rock on the edge of the pine forest. There had
been talk of a cattle-killer in the valley, of a
leopard and other animals displaced by the
construction of the dam at Tehri. The blasting of
hillsides and the felling of trees had forced them
out of the forest.

Suddenly, there was a babble of voices and a

surge of excitement at one end of the village street. Nathu, a cowherd, was running down the street waving a strip of red cloth as though it were a flag. Every now and then he stopped to show it to a passer-by.

"I found it hanging from a bush!" he exclaimed. "There's blood on it, see?"

"Mr Mani wears red pyjamas," said someone.

Could he have been seized and eaten? If so,

where were his remains? And why had he been in his pyjamas?

Bina and Sonu and the rest of the children had followed their teachers into the school playground. Feeling a little lost, Bina looked around for Prakash. She turned, and found herself facing a dark, slender young woman wearing spectacles. The woman looked too old to be another pupil – but only just. She had a kind, expressive face. Bina noticed too that she had lovely hands – they certainly hadn't been used for milking cows or working in the fields.

"Are you new here too?" said the young woman, smiling.

"Yes, we're from Koli."

"It's a long walk from Koli – you didn't see any leopards, did you?" Bina shook her head solemnly, but the young woman was still smiling. "What year are you in?" she said.

"The sixth."

"Then I'm your new teacher. My name is Tania Ramola. Come along, let's go and see if we can settle down in our classroom."

Mr Mani turned up at twelve o'clock, wondering what all the fuss was about. No, he snapped, he had not been attacked by a leopard; and yes, he *had* been walking in the forest in his pyjamas, and what was so strange about that? Pyjamas were more comfortable than trousers.

"But they got caught in a wretched raspberry bush," he grumbled.

So it wasn't blood on his pyjamas, just raspberry juice! (Mr Mani had a weakness for raspberries.) He finally admitted that he'd gone further than he had intended, and lost his way coming back – Mr Mani was getting more absent-minded than ever.

CHAPTER THREE

Leopard on the Prowl

Bina enjoyed her first day at the new school. She felt at ease with Miss Ramola, as did most of the girls and boys in her class. Tania Ramola told them a lot about herself. She had been to distant towns such as Delhi and Lucknow – places the children had only heard about. She told them about her brother, who was a pilot and flew planes all over the world.

"Will he fly over Nauti some day?" Bina asked.

"Perhaps he will!" replied Miss Ramola.

Most of the children had of course seen planes flying overhead, but none of them had seen a ship, and only a few had been in a train. Their mountain was a great distance from the railway and hundreds of miles from the sea.

Bina, Sonu and Prakash had company for part of the way home, but gradually the other children went off in different directions. After crossing the stream, the three children were on their own again.

It was a steep climb all the way back to their village. Prakash had a supply of peanuts which he shared with Bina and Sonu, and at a small spring they quenched their thirst.

When they were less than a mile from home, they met a postman who had finished his round of the villages in the area and was now returning to Nauti.

"Don't waste time along the way," he told them. "Try to get home before dark."

"What's the hurry?" asked Prakash, glancing at his watch. "It's only five o'clock."

"There's a leopard on the prowl. I saw it this morning, not far from the stream. So don't take any chances. Get home early."

"So there really is a leopard," said Sonu. "I hope it's not a man-eater!"

They took the postman's advice and walked faster, and Sonu forgot to complain about his aching feet. They were all home before sunset.

There was a smell of cooking in the air and they were hungry.

"Cabbage and chapattis," said Prakash gloomily. "But I could eat anything today." He stopped outside his small slate-roofed house, and Bina and Sonu waved goodbye and carried on across a couple of ploughed fields until they reached their own stone dwelling.

Their mother was lighting the kitchen stove. They greeted her with great hugs and demands for immediate food. She was a good cook who could make even the simplest of dishes taste delicious.

Electricity had yet to reach their village, and they took their meal by the light of a kerosene lamp. After the meal, Sonu settled down to do a little homework, while Bina stepped outside to look at the stars.

Across the fields, someone was playing a flute. "It must be Prakash," thought Bina. "He always breaks off on the high notes." But the flute music was simple and appealing, and she began singing softly to herself in the dark.

CHAPTER FOUR

Fear on the Mountain

Mr Mani was having trouble with the porcupines. They had been getting into his garden at night and digging up and eating his potatoes. From his bedroom window - left open now that the mild April weather had arrived – he could listen to them enjoying the vegetables he had worked so hard to grow. Scrunch, scrunch, *katar, katar*, as their sharp teeth sliced through the largest and juiciest of potatoes. The sound made Mr Mani tremble with rage and indignation. Yes, Mr Mani hated porcupines.

Mr Mani got out of bed every night, torch in one hand, a stout stick in the other, but as soon as he stepped into the garden the crunching and digging stopped. He would grope around in the dark, swinging wildly with the stick, but not a single porcupine was to be seen or heard. As soon as he was back in bed – they seemed to know instinctively when he had gone – the sounds would start all over again. Scrunch,

scrunch, *katar*, *katar* ...

Mr Mani would come to his class tired
and dishevelled, with rings beneath his eyes and
a permanent frown on his face. It took some
time for his pupils to discover the reason for his
misery. Though they laughed at first, they felt
sorry for Mr Mani and took to discussing how
his potatoes could be saved from the porcupines.

To everyone's surprise, it was Prakash who came up with the idea of a moat or water-ditch.

"Porcupines don't like water," he said knowledgeably.

"How do you know?" asked one of his friends.

"Throw water on one and see how it runs!"

There was no-one who could disprove Prakash's theory, and the class fell in with the

idea of building a moat, especially as it meant getting most of the day off school.

Armed with spades and shovels collected from all parts of the village, the pupils from Class 6 took up their positions around Mr Mani's potato field and began digging a ditch.

After several hours the moat was ready, and Prakash and the others managed to divert the

water from a stream that flowed past the village. They had the satisfaction of watching it flow gently into the ditch. Everyone went home in a good mood. By nightfall, the ditch had overflowed, the potato field was flooded, and Mr Mani found himself marooned inside his house. But Prakash and his friends had won the day. The porcupines stayed away *that* night!

A month had passed, and wild violets, daisies and buttercups now sprinkled the hill slopes. On her way to school, Bina gathered enough to make a little posy. The bunch of flowers fitted easily into an old inkwell. Miss Ramola was delighted to find this little display in the middle of her desk.

"Who put these here?" she asked in surprise.

Bina kept quiet. The rest of the class smiled secretively.

After that, they took turns bringing flowers for Miss Ramola.

On her long walks to school and home again, Bina became aware that May was truly the 'month of new leaf', as her mother said. The oak leaves were bright green above and silver beneath, and when they rippled in the breeze, they were clouds of silvery green. The path was strewn with old leaves, dry and crackly. Sonu loved kicking them around.

One morning, they saw clouds of white butterflies floating across the stream. Sonu was chasing a butterfly when he stumbled over something dark and repulsive. He shouted and went sprawling on the grass. When he got to his feet, he looked round to see what had tripped him up – and saw the awful remains of a half-eaten animal.

"Bina! Prakash!" he shouted.

It was a dead sheep, killed some days earlier, obviously by a much larger animal.

"Only a leopard could have done this," said Prakash, his face suddenly pale.

"Let's get away," said Sonu. "It might still be around!"

Bina took him by the hand. "Leopards don't

attack humans," she said, trying to sound calm.

"They will, if they once get a taste for us!" insisted Prakash.

"Well, this one hasn't attacked any people yet," said Bina, although she couldn't really be sure. Hadn't Mr Mani said there had been rumours of a leopard attacking some workers near the dam? But she didn't want to frighten Sonu, so she kept quiet.

"It's probably come here because of all the blasting near the dam," said Prakash. "That's what Mr Mani says."

They hurried home, silently, all three feeling threatened by the leopard's presence. And for a few days, whenever they reached the stream, they crossed over very quickly, unwilling to linger there long.

CHAPTER FIVE

+=====+

Journey to the Dam

Mr Mani was right. A few days earlier some workers had been attacked near the dam site. They had driven the leopard off, but one of the men had been badly clawed and was now in hospital at Tehri. Perhaps it was the same leopard that was now prowling around the villages.

Mr Mani didn't think much of the dam.

"First they displaced all the village people in the area – including my uncle's family – and now they're driving away all the wildlife. Herds of deer have been seen moving southwards. What does that leave for a leopard to eat? Just our dogs and our sheep. And if you get in its way, it will go for you!" he added pointedly, looking at Prakash.

Prakash laughed nervously. But Miss Ramola came to the defence of the dam.

"It'll bring electricity to all our villages," she said. "The school will have lights and so will our homes. And there'll be water for the fields all the way to Delhi."

"Oh yes, to Delhi," said Mr Mani, bitterly. "But it won't reach *our* fields. Rivers flow downhill, not uphill!"

The argument was taking place on the classroom verandah, and Bina, who had been listening carefully, remarked that she had yet to see the dam – for that matter, none of the children had seen it!

"Well, why don't we visit Tehri and look at it?" said Miss Ramola brightly. "What do you think, Mr Mani? We could take both our classes to see the dam."

Mr Mani had seemed reluctant at first, but then it occurred to him that it might be a good thing for his pupils to see for themselves what was happening . . . and besides, it would give him a chance to look up some old friends. The headmaster thought the trip was a great idea, and gave his permission gladly. And if all the children contributed five rupees each, he'd arrange for a bus to take them to Tehri.

It was Bina's first visit to a large town – her first
bus ride!

The sharp curves along the winding,
downhill road made several children feel sick.
The bus driver seemed to be in a tearing hurry.
He took them along at a rolling, rollicking
speed, which made Bina feel quite giddy. She
rested her head on her arms and refused to look
out of the window. Hairpin bends and cliff
edges, pine forests and snow-capped peaks all
swept past her, but she felt too ill to want to look

at anything. It was just as well – those sudden
drops, hundreds of feet to the valley below, were
quite frightening. Bina began to wish that she
hadn't come!

Miss Ramola and Mr Mani didn't seem to
notice the lurching and groaning of the old bus.
They had made this journey many times. They
were busy arguing about the dam – an argument
that was to continue on and off for much of the
day – Miss Ramola calmly pointing out the
advantages, and Mr Mani dismissing them

crossly. At one point, Prakash butted in to ask if they would be able to go fishing on the dam waters. Both teachers looked at him blankly – they hadn't thought of that!

Bina felt better when the road levelled out near Tehri. As they crossed an old bridge over the wide river, they were startled by a tremendous bang which made the bus shudder. A cloud of dust rose above the town.

"They're blasting the mountain," said Miss Ramola.

"The end of a mountain," said Mr Mani, mournfully.

While they were drinking cups of tea at the bus stop, Miss Ramola and Mr Mani continued their argument. While Miss Ramola talked of all the benefits that the dam would bring to large numbers of people, Mr Mani declared that it was a menace. He had a new argument. This was an earthquake zone – just think of the terrible disaster if there was an earthquake and the dam burst!

"An earthquake!" exclaimed Prakash. "Will the mountains crumble?"

"No, but the dam will," said Mr Mani.

Bina found it all very confusing. She thought of the leopard.

"What about the animals in the mountains – what will happen to them?" she asked.

"Many will perish," said Mr Mani, gloomily.

"Many will find new homes," said Miss Ramola.

"Oh yes – in our school, perhaps," said Mr Mani, feeling he had won the argument.

CHAPTER SIX

Last Days of Tehri Town

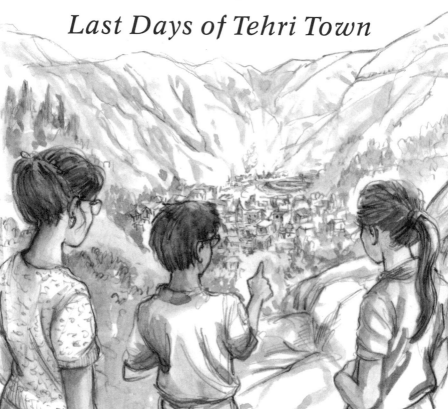

Tania Ramola and her group had taken the steep road to the hill above Tehri. Half an hour's climbing brought them to a little plateau which overlooked the town, the river and the dam site.

The earthworks for the dam were only just

beginning to rise from the ground, but a wide tunnel had been bored through the mountain to divert the river into another channel. Down below, the old town was still spread out across the valley and from a distance it looked quite charming and picturesque.

"Will the whole town be swallowed up by the waters of the dam?" asked Bina. She looked down at the clock tower and the old palace. She saw what she took to be schools and temples. There were hundreds of houses stretching for what looked like miles up the valley.

"Yes, all of it," said Miss Ramola. "All the people will have to go – but they'll be resettled elsewhere. There's a new town being built for them, sixty miles from here."

"But the town's been here for hundreds of years," said Bina. "The people have been quite happy without the dam, haven't they?"

"I suppose they have. But the dam isn't just for them – it's for the millions who live further downstream, across the plains."

"And doesn't it matter what happens to this place?"

"The local people will be given new homes

somewhere else, Bina."

Miss Ramola found herself on the defensive and decided to change the subject. "Everyone must be hungry. It's time we had our lunch."

Bina kept quiet. She didn't think the local people would want to go away. And it was a good thing, she mused, that there was only a small stream running past her village, and not a big river that people might want to build a dam on. To be uprooted like that – a town and hundreds of villages – and put down somewhere on the hot, dusty plains – seemed to her unbearable.

Well, I'm glad *I* don't live in Tehri, she thought.

She didn't know it but, though most of the people of Tehri remained in their homes for the present, most of the animals and birds had already left the area – the leopard among them.

Prakash, who was with Mr Mani's group, thought the lake behind the dam would be a great place to go rowing, once it was ready. But right now he was more interested in the sweet shops that tempted him on all sides with their glass cases full of golden *jalebies* and syrupy *gulab-jamuns*.

Bina kept close to Miss Ramola as they all walked through the colourful, crowded bazaar, where fruit-sellers did business beside silversmiths, and pavement vendors sold everything from umbrellas to glass bangles. Sparrows attacked sacks of grain, monkeys made off with bananas, and stray cows and dogs rummaged in overflowing refuse bins, but nobody took any notice. Music blared out from radios and loudspeakers. Buses blew their horns. Bina came to the conclusion that townspeople loved lots of noise.

Sonu bought a whistle to add to the general din, but Miss Ramola told him to put it away. He wasn't really supposed to be on the trip, but nobody had noticed him following Bina onto the bus. Bina had brought five rupees that she'd saved, and now she used them to buy a cheap cotton head-scarf for her mother.

As they were about to enter a small restaurant for a meal, they met up with Prakash and his companions; but of Mr Mani there was no sign.

"He must have met one of his relatives," said Prakash. "He has relatives everywhere."

They walked the length of the bazaar without seeing Mr Mani. At last, when they were about to give up the search, they saw him emerge from a by-lane, a large sack slung over his shoulder.

"Sir, where have you been?" asked Prakash. "We've been looking for you everywhere."

On Mr Mani's face was a look of triumph.

"Help me with this bag," he said breathlessly.

"You've bought more potatoes, sir," said Prakash.

"Not potatoes, boy. Dahlia bulbs!"

Miss Ramola took her group back to the restaurant. The tables were dirty, the floor unswept – all of a piece with the general air of neglect about the town. After all, everyone in Tehri would have to move before long.

Bina had no appetite for her food. Sonu, on the other hand, tucked into his dal and rice with gusto – he was hungry!

So was Prakash, on the other side of the street, where Mr Mani had found a rival restaurant for his group – just as scruffy, but offering a wider variety of dishes. Prakash enjoyed his vegetable koftas, followed by a warm, sweet, sticky *gulab-jamun*.

Across the street, Bina stared out of the restaurant window – she was looking forward to going home to her mother's clean kitchen and the fresh air around her mountain home. She didn't like the heat, dust and noise of this crowded valley town. Perhaps it was the right place for a dam, after all!

CHAPTER SEVEN

Leopard by the Stream

It was dark by the time they were all back in Nauti.

Bina did not feel so ill on the return journey. Going uphill was definitely better than going downhill. But, by the time the bus reached Nauti, it was too late for most of the children to walk back to the more distant villages. Most of

the boys were put up in different homes, while the girls were given beds on the school verandah.

The night was warm and still. Large moths fluttered around the single lamp that lit the verandah. Counting moths, Sonu soon fell asleep. But Bina stayed awake for some time, listening to the sounds of the night. A nightjar went *tonk-tonk* in the bushes, and somewhere in the forest an owl hooted softly. The sharp call of a barking-deer travelled up the valley, from

the direction of the stream. Jackals kept howling. It seemed that there were more of them than ever before.

Bina was not the only one to hear the barking-deer. The leopard, stretched full-length on a rocky ledge, heard it too. The leopard raised its head and then got up slowly. The deer was its natural prey, but there weren't many left in this area. So the leopard had taken to attacking dogs and cattle near the villages. The villagers no longer allowed their cattle to stray far, and at night they were securely locked into their sheds. Favourite dogs, used to roaming the village streets at night, were now called indoors before sunset. Children did not play out of doors after dark.

As the sound of the barking-deer's cry grew louder, the leopard left its look-out point and moved swiftly through the shadows towards the stream.

CHAPTER EIGHT

Landslide!

In early June the hills were dry and dusty, and forest fires broke out, destroying shrubs and trees, killing birds and small animals. The resin in the pines made them burn fiercely, and the wind would take sparks from the trees and carry them into the dry grass and leaves, so that new fires would spring up before the old ones had died out. Fortunately, Bina's village was not in the pine belt; the fires did not reach it. But Nauti was surrounded by a fire that raged for three days, and the children had to stay away from school. Naturally the leopard stayed away from Nauti too.

And then, towards the end of June, the monsoon rains arrived and there was an end to forest fires. For the next three months, the lower Himalayas would be drenched in rain, mist and cloud.

The first rain arrived while Bina, Prakash and Sonu were returning home from school.

Those first few drops on the dusty path made them cry out with excitement. Then the rain grew heavier and a wonderful aroma rose from the earth.

"The best smell in the world!" exclaimed Bina.

Everything suddenly came to life - the grass, the crops, the birds. Even the leaves on the trees glistened and looked new.

That first wet weekend, Bina and Sonu helped their mother plant beans, maize and cucumbers. Sometimes, when the rain was very heavy, they had to run indoors. Otherwise, they worked in the rain, the soft mud clinging to their bare legs.

Prakash now owned a dog, a black dog called Raja, with one ear up and one ear down. Prakash said Raja was a very clever dog and that he would protect the village from the leopard. But Raja just ran around barking and getting in everyone's way.

In Nauti, Tania Ramola was trying to find a dry spot in the quarters she'd been given. It was an old building and the roof was leaking in several places. Mugs and buckets were scattered about the floor to catch the drips.

Mr Mani had dug up all his remaining potatoes and presented them to the friends and neighbours who had often shared their breakfasts or dinners with him. He was now having a wonderful time planting dahlia bulbs all over his garden.

"Watch out for those porcupines!" warned his sister.

＋≋＋

Now when the children crossed the stream, they found that the water level had risen by about a foot. Small cascades had turned into waterfalls. Ferns had sprung up on the banks. Frogs chanted.

Prakash and his dog dashed across the stream. Bina and Sonu followed more cautiously. The current was much stronger now and the water was almost up to their knees. Once they had crossed the stream, they hurried along the path, anxious not to be caught in a sudden downpour.

By the time they reached school, each of them had two or three leeches clinging to their legs. They had to use salt to remove them. For the children, the leeches were the most troublesome thing about the rainy season. The leopard was bothered by them too. It couldn't lie in the long grass without getting leeches on its paws and face.

One day, Bina, Prakash and Sonu were about to cross the stream when they heard a low rumble, which grew louder every second. Looking up at the opposite hill, they saw several trees shudder, tilt outwards and begin to fall. Earth and rocks bulged out from the mountain, then came crashing down into the ravine.

"Landslide!" shouted Sonu.

"It's carried away the path!" cried Bina. "Don't go any further."

There was a tremendous roar as more rocks, trees and bushes fell away and crashed down the hillside.

Prakash's dog, who had gone ahead, came running back, his tail between his legs.

They remained rooted to the spot until the rocks had stopped falling and the dust had settled. Birds circled the area, calling wildly.

A frightened barking-deer ran past them.

"We can't go to school now," said Prakash. "There's no way around."

They turned and trudged home through the gathering mist.

CHAPTER NINE

Those Fierce Yellow Eyes

For several days, the children couldn't get to school. Bina missed their long walks. She wanted to see her school friends and Miss Ramola. Prakash didn't really mind not going to school, but he didn't like feeling helpless just because their path had been swept away. So he

explored the hillside until he found a goat track going around the mountain. It joined up with another path near Nauti. This made their walk longer by about a mile, but Bina didn't mind. It was much cooler now that the rains were in full swing.

One day, on their way along the goat track, Prakash's dog Raja had, as usual, run ahead barking. Then, suddenly, he came dashing back, whimpering.

"He's always running away from something," observed Sonu.

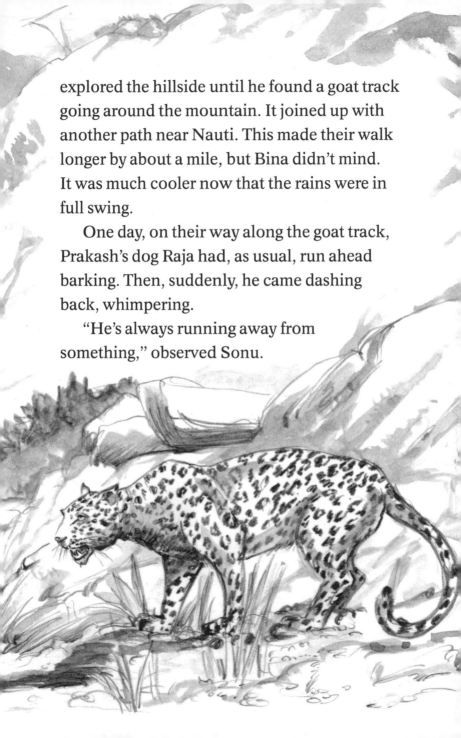

But a minute later, he understood the reason for Raja's fear. They rounded a bend, and saw the leopard, standing in their way. It was staring straight at them. They were hypnotised by its fierce yellow eyes.

The dog had disappeared, but all three children were petrified – their fear rooted them to the spot. A low growl rose from the leopard's throat. It seemed ready to spring.

The children stood perfectly still, afraid to move or say a word. The snarling leopard stared at them for a few seconds, twitched its tail, then bounded across the path and into the oak forest.

Sonu was shaking. Bina could hear her heart hammering.

"Did you . . . did you see the way he sprang?" stammered Prakash. "And wasn't he beautiful?"

When they finally got to school, Prakash couldn't stop talking about the leopard – he forgot to look at his watch for the rest of the day.

For a few days, the forest ranger, armed with a gun, accompanied them on the path near the stream. The one day, as they were on their way home, Sonu stopped and pointed to a large outcrop of rock on the next hill.

The leopard stood far above them, outlined against the sky – it looked powerful, majestic. Standing beside it were two young cubs.

"Look at those little ones!" exclaimed Sonu.

"So it's a 'she', not a 'he'," said Prakash.

"That's why she was killing so often," said Bina. "She had her cubs to feed."

They remained still for several minutes, gazing up at the leopard and her cubs. The leopard family took no notice of them.

"She knows we're here," said Prakash, "but she doesn't mind. She knows we won't harm them."

"I wonder if it's because she knows we're cubs too," said Sonu.

CHAPTER TEN

Singing on the Mountain

It was the end of September. The rains were coming to an end, and there was a chill in the air – winter was not far away. The landslide had been cleared, and Bina, Prakash and Sonu could once again cross their stream.

Prakash had learnt to play the flute quite well, and he played it on the way to school and then again on the way home. As a result, he didn't look at his watch so often any more.

One day, they found a small crowd in front of Mr Mani's house.

"What could have happened?" wondered Bina. "I hope he hasn't got lost again," she said, thinking of the leopard and her cubs.

"Maybe he's sick," said Sonu.

"Maybe it's the porcupines," smiled Prakash.

But it was none of these things. Mr Mani's first dahlia was in bloom. It was a huge red one – no-one had ever seen such a magnificent flower!

Mr Mani was a happy man. And his mood only improved over the following week, as more and more dahlias flowered – red, crimson, yellow, purple and white. One even appeared on Tania Ramola's desk. He got on with her quite well now, and they often stopped to talk about their pupils. They still argued about the dam, but they understood each other more now and could disagree without taking offence.

On their way home one day, Bina, Prakash and Sonu talked about what they might do when they grew up.

"I think I'll become a teacher," said Bina. "I'll teach children about animals and birds, and trees and flowers."

"Especially about leopards!" said Prakash.

"I'm going to be a pilot," said Sonu. "I want to fly a plane like Miss Ramola's brother."

"And what about you, Prakash?" asked Bina.

Prakash just smiled and said, "Maybe I'll be a flute player," and he put the flute to his lips and played a sweet melody.

"Well, the world needs flute players too," said Bina, as they fell into step beside him.

The leopard had been stalking a wild mountain goat – her young ones were growing quickly. She paused when she heard the flute and the voices of the children.

Bina and the two boys started singing their favourite song again.

Five more miles to go!
We climb through rain and snow,
A river to cross –
A mountain to pass –
Now we've four more miles to go!

The leopard waited until they had passed, before returning to the trail of the mountain goat.